SCOTT & JESUS

LOST COMEDY DUO OF THE SCRIPTURES

ANOTHER BOOK OF INAPPROPRIATE HUMOR

BY STEVE CASE

THE APOCRYPHILE PRESS
BERKELEY, CA

apocryphile press
BERKELEY, CA

Apocryphile Press
1700 Shattuck Ave #81
Berkeley, CA 94709
www.apocryphile.org

Printed in the United States of America
ISBN 978-1-949643-11-4

An Introduction by Scott the Almost Apostle

To begin at the beginning.

The world was without form and the spirit of God...

No, not that beginning. I"m just kidding.

To begin, I harbor Jesus no ill will. We really did try and make a go of it, but it just wasn't his style. He gave it a shot.

Also, I take no exception to the "almost apostle" nickname. We tried. He went his way, and I went mine. Considering everything he went through I'm thinking I got the better part of the deal. My hecklers threw rotten vegetables at the most. His? Well, you know what happened to him. He didn't offer me a spot on the team, but I would have turned him down anyway. I think his mother had a hand in that too.

We were friends in school. The teacher assigned us a book report and we did it as a routine and we killed. Then after school, he went back to work at his dad's shop. Jesus was an adequate carpenter at best. Chairs or tables, he was your guy. Anything ornate like a wardrobe or china cabinet and he was lost. Which was okay because nobody had china.

Like a lot of us in those days, he went into his father's business. We all did. He did it because his dad did. His step-dad I mean, not his real dad. I guess he went into that business for the same reason.

We were both about 30, and he hadn't started preaching yet, but he was a natural in front of a crowd. He had a real gift. We started working and got a few gigs right away in Jerusalem. The Swartz wedding reception was a crowd pleaser. We worked a few clubs opening for this guy, named Schecky who did comedy prophecies. The irony was a lot of his stuff came true. Not until long after his death of course but still.

Jesus started slipping his longer bits into the act. Real heady stuff. He called them parables. A lot of it made no sense, and I kept telling him these were not the obscure comedy audiences. These people liked slipping on a pile of camel dung and a round of Who's on Eyns.

Plus his mother wasn't keen on the whole act. She kept telling him he was better than the act. What she meant was, he could do better than me. He could do better on his own.

That wedding story you read about in the gospels? That was our last gig. We were slated to work the room, me pretending to be an old rabbi and Jesus would come in with a bit about circumcision. Funny stuff. But the Kaminsky's ran out of wine. Jesus's mom got him by the ear and took him to the kitchen. The next thing we know there's plenty of wine at our duo is done.

Like I said, I bear him no grudge. He really found his schtick after that. So we parted ways.

Somebody found a bunch of our old bits and decided to publish them. So here they are. Some are pretty rough. Some were totally improvised in the moment. And you won't find any of it in your Vacation Bible School curriculum, but we had a good run.

Here they are...the lost bits.

Scott
(the almost apostle)

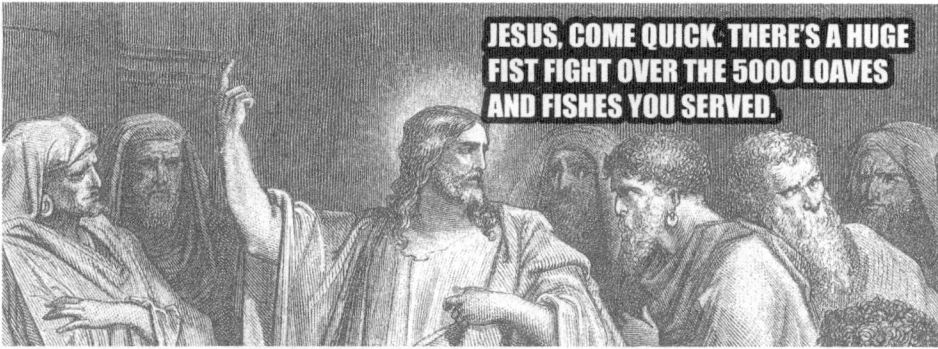

NEVER ARGUE WITH SOMEONE IN A TENT...

BECAUSE WHEN YOU STORM OUT, YOU CAN'T SLAM A FLAP.

UMMMM... NO

WHADAYA THINK...NEW COMMANDMENT?

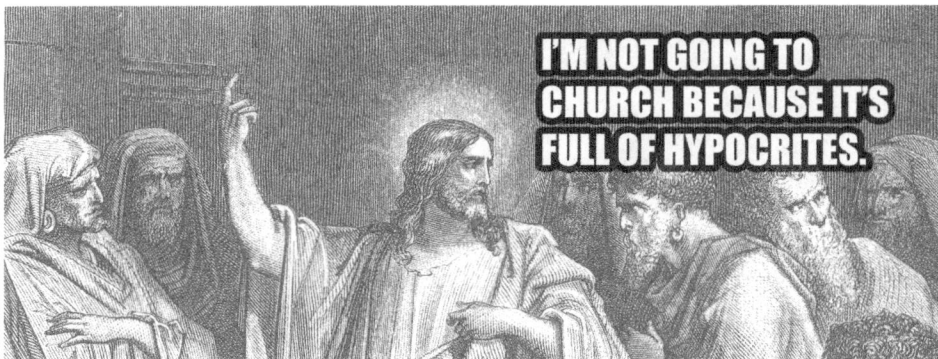

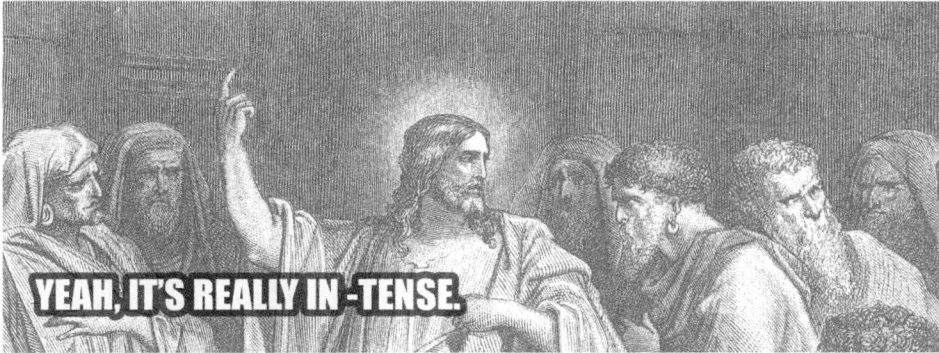

jesus and scott: lost comedy duo of the scriptures

steve case presents

SO, JOHN TRIED TO CROSS THE JORDAN RIVER SINGLE-HANDEDLY.

BUT HE JUST SORT OF SPUN AROUND IN CIRCLES.

WE'RE ALL A LITTLE WORRIED ABOUT JOHN.

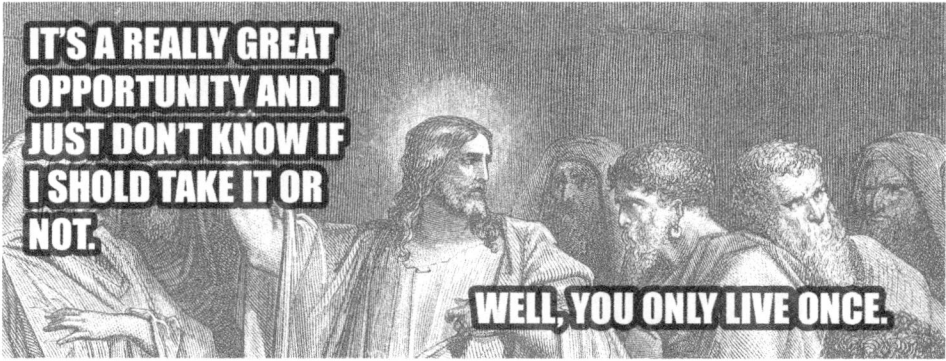

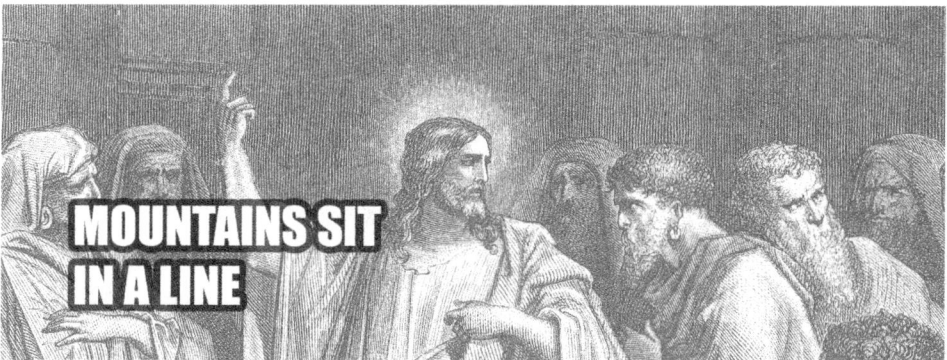

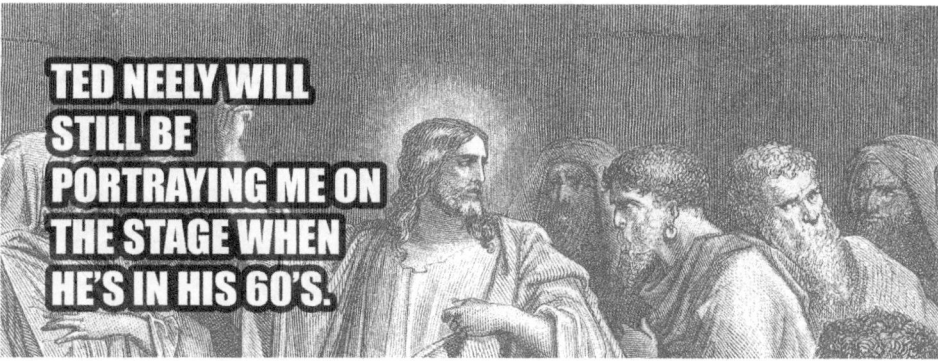

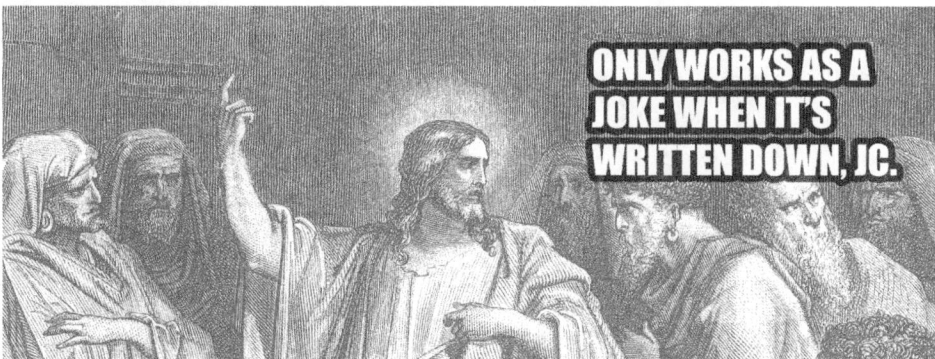

ONCE THERE WAS A MAN WHO SENT HIS SON INTO THE CITY TO BUY A CANDLE HOLDER...

THE SON RETURNED WITH A CAKE.

OH, JESUS.

'NUTHER PARABLE.

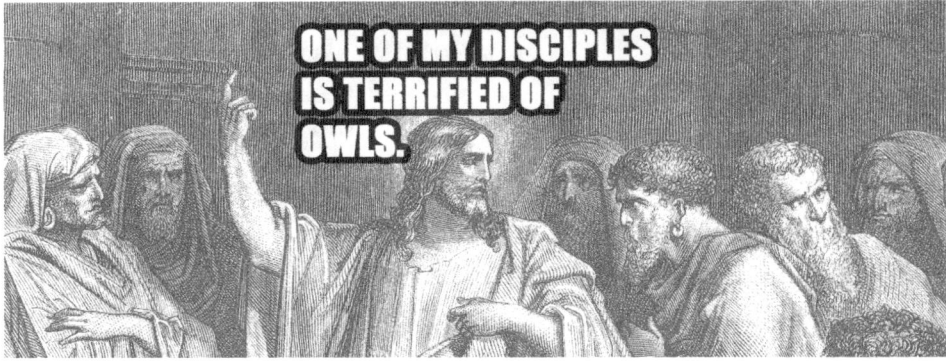

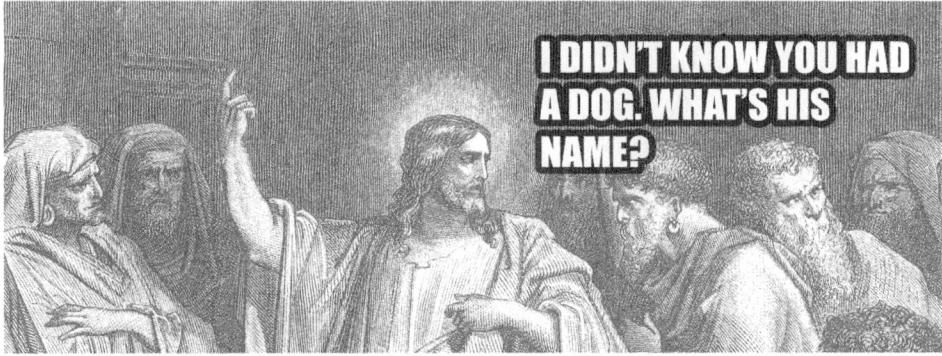

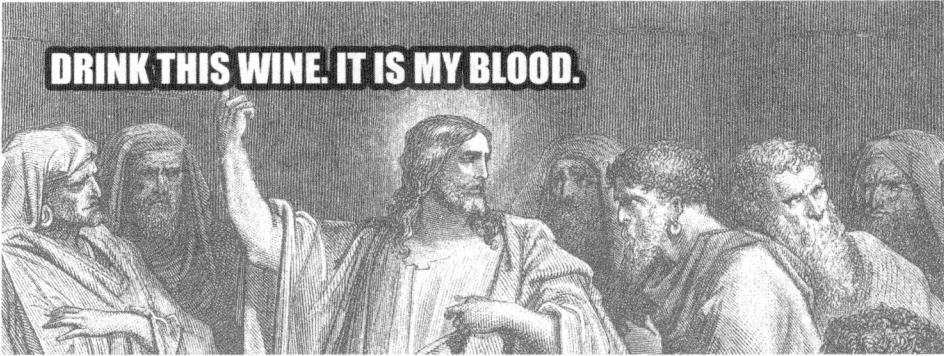

69

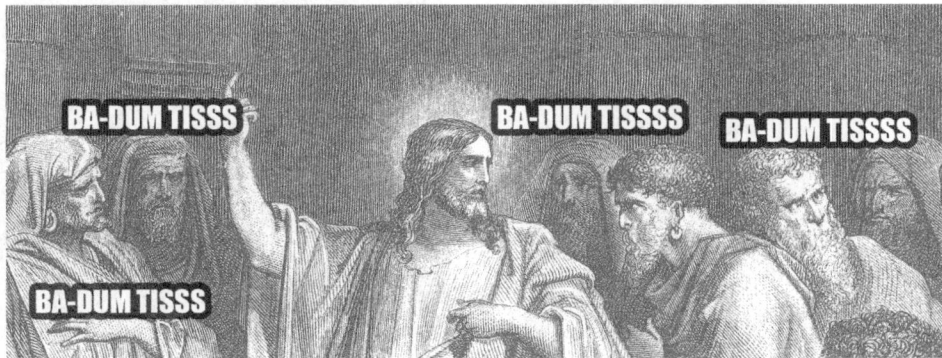

GET ALL OF STEVE CASE'S
GREAT ADVENTURES IN INAPPROPRIATE HUMOR

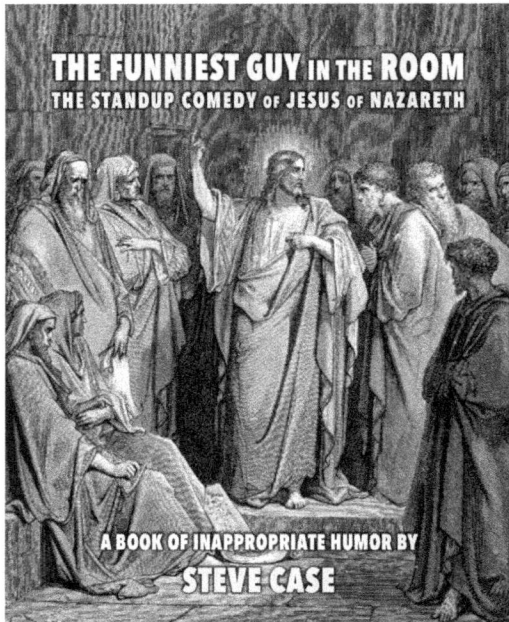

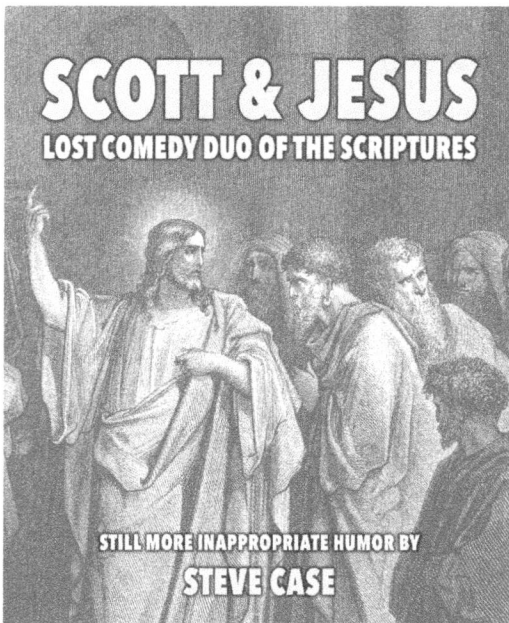
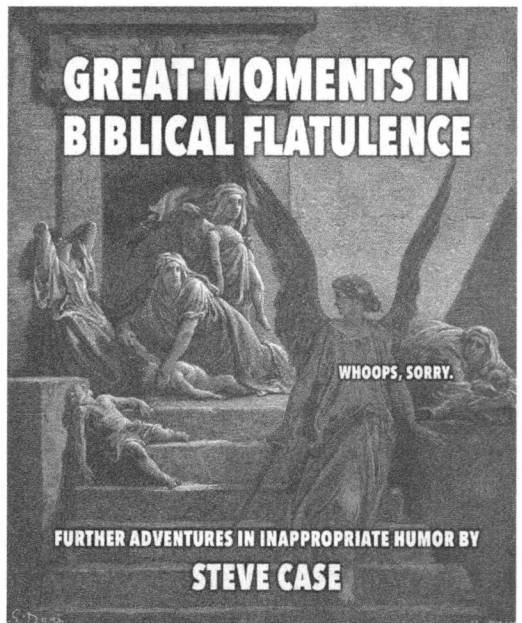

www.ingramcontent.com/pod-product-compliance
Lightning Source LLC
Chambersburg PA
CBHW081419090426
42738CB00017B/3424